Human and Divine

A PERSONAL PILGRIMAGE TO MEDJUGORJE

To My Dear Friend Lesley.

At last my little book has been published. It is a tribute to my dear mother who would have been 100 yrs old on the 29th June the Feast of St. Peter and Paul.

And to thank you for your kindness to me when I lived in Arundel. Thank you

Human and Divine

A PERSONAL PILGRIMAGE TO MEDJUGORJE

———⚬○⚬———

from your friend

MRS - Pamela J Hill

PJ Hill

ATHENA PRESS
LONDON

26th August 2008.

Human and Divine
A Personal Pilgrimage to Medjugorje
Copyright © Pamela J Hill 2008

All Rights Reserved

No part of this book may be reproduced in any form
by photocopying or by any electronic or mechanical means,
including information storage or retrieval systems,
without permission in writing from both the copyright
owner and the publisher of this book.

ISBN 978 1 84748 302 7

First published 2008 by
ATHENA PRESS
Queen's House, 2 Holly Road
Twickenham TW1 4EG
United Kingdom

Printed for Athena Press

Mrs Jennie Newley (née Sarah Jane Hughes)

Born 29 June 1908 in Glencormac, County Wicklow, Ireland

Died 28 February 1993 in London aged eighty-four years

This book is dedicated to my darling loving mother with my profound love and thanks for all she was and did for us and the sacrifices that only a mother can make for her children, and without whom I would never have gone to Medjugorje.

When I went on pilgrimage to Medjugorje in
Yugoslavia (now Bosnia and Herzegovina) with the
Centre for Peace
from 26 May to 3 June 1991, I was asked if I would
share my experience with my parish.

I wrote the following as monthly instalments
in the parish newsletter.

―――――○◯○―――――

Contents

CHAPTER ONE
What is Medjugorje?
11

CHAPTER TWO
Medjugorje Continued
16

CHAPTER THREE
Father Jozo
21

CHAPTER FOUR
Our Lady
27

CHAPTER FIVE
Mount Križevac – Cross Mountain
32

CHAPTER SIX
Cross Mountain Continued
38

CHAPTER SEVEN
Obracenje (Conversion)
43

OBSERVATIONS
50

EPILOGUE
54

Chapter One

WHAT IS MEDJUGORJE?

Until recently, Medjugorje, a village in the commune of Čitluk in western Herzegovina – historic Brotnjo (Broćnjo) – was unknown even in its own country. Nothing distinguished it from the other villages and settlements of the region; nothing that would justify its fame now.

Medjugorje, the largest of the five villages (the others being Bijakovici, Vionica, Miletina and Šurmanci), gave its name to the large Roman Catholic parish, but even that is not enough to justify its fame.

In recent years, Medjugorje has become one of the most famous and most visited centres of pilgrimage in the whole Catholic world. On 24 June 1981 the Blessed Virgin Mary, mother of Jesus, appeared in the village of Bijakovici in the Medjugorje parish to six young parishioners (two boys and four girls – Marija, Mirjana, Jakov aged sixteen, Ivanka aged fifteen, Vicka aged seventeen, and Ivan aged sixteen). There have been apparitions every day since that date and thousands upon thousands of pilgrims from all over the world have been converging on Medjugorje – thirteen million between the years 1981 (when the first apparition was recorded) and 1991 alone. Most of these pilgrims are from abroad rather than from Bosnia Herzegovina itself. The word 'Medjugorje' in Slavic means 'the region in between two mountains'.

My mother had been to Medjugorje in 1989 and felt that Our Lady was calling her back. She had been so impressed with Medjugorje that she knew she must return. She decided to arrange her own pilgrimage. At the time, she was eighty-two years old, wheelchair-bound and completely paralysed on one side from a stroke ten years previously. Because Medjugorje had not yet been recognised by the Church, priests were not allowed to organise parish pilgrimages. My mother asked me to go with her. I tried to persuade her not to go as I thought it would be too much for her, but she was determined to do it and so I went to help her and look after her. She gathered together fourteen further people who wanted to go: two nuns from her parish – Sister Martina and Sister Eileen; a couple in their seventies – Alice, who was in a wheelchair but could stand and walk a little and had not been out of her house for two years, and her husband Eric who was determined to get her there; Sheena (fifteen months old – our youngest member) and her mum Sarah; Judi who was expecting her eighth child; an Anglican lady called Margaret; a widow named Kitty who had no children and whose husband had died the day after he retired; a husband and wife named Frank and Anne with their twenty-seven-year-old mentally handi-capped son Tony; a lovely Italian lady called Anna; and finally Monica, who had recently returned to the Church after a long lapse following the death of her son in a car crash, and who turned out to be the younger sister of my chief bridesmaid thirty-seven years previously. Our pilgrimage was organised through the Centre for Peace.

The whole message of Medjugorje is peace (MIR). While at Lourdes Our Lady said, 'I am the Immaculate Conception', here she says, 'I am the Queen of Peace.' Our Lady asks us for five things at Medjugorje:

1. Prayer of the Rosary, prayer of the heart;
2. Eucharist;
3. Bible;
4. Fasting;
5. Monthly confession.

Our Lady asks us to say fifteen decades of the Rosary every day. But she also adds, 'It is better to say one Hail Mary with the heart than fifteen decades with no heart.' As well as this she asks us to read the Bible every day. When she appears to the visionaries holding the Bible she is crying, and says, 'How much time do you spend watching television and reading newspapers, and how much time reading the Bible?' We are also asked to fast on bread and water every Wednesday and Friday. But she stresses not to do this if we are sick or have health problems. Monthly confession is also suggested. Our Lady says, 'We have got too used to our sins and do not think them sins any longer.'

People who come to Medjugorje feel they are loved, which makes any differences between people disappear, annulled by love. These are the true United Nations – founded on love, not by decree and the signature of state representatives. Here, true ecumenism is at work and something of what Paul of Tarsus said is coming true: 'There are no more Jews and Greeks, no more slaves and freemen, no more men and women. Because we are all one (Galatians 3:28).

Referring to the Rosary again, which Our Lady has asked us to say, She states, 'Dear children, I ask you to ask everyone to pray the Rosary; with rosaries in your hands you will conquer and will overcome all the troubles which Satan is trying to inflict on the Catholic Church.' Our Lady gave this message to Marija Pavlovic on Tuesday 25 June 1985 when she asked, 'Our Lady, what do you wish to say to priests?'

'Let all priests pray the Rosary. Give time to the Rosary,' she replied.

Over the past twenty or more years we have uncritically accepted the deceitful suggestion that it is a 'boring' prayer because it is repetitive. Yet practice is proving us wrong. The repetition has a stilling effect but it also has a unifying one. It concentrates our being – not just our minds but our hearts. The Rosary, we now appreciate, is a superb prayer of the heart. It does not make sense to describe it as 'boring' because it is a prayer at a higher level than intelligence – the level of love. That is why someone who says 'I love the Rosary', without knowing why, has the Holy Spirit praying in their heart. And in the Rosary we meditate on the whole life of Christ and the Coming of the Holy Spirit to the Crowning of Our Blessed Lady.

At Saint James' Church in Medjugorje at 6 p.m. every evening all nationalities gather to say the Rosary and Litany and sing hymns. Mass is said in five languages at 7 a.m. every morning. The English Mass is at 10 a.m. and is concelebrated by no less than thirty priests all from different countries; there are usually between thirty and a hundred priests in Medjugorje at any one time. At Medjugorje, you are impressed by the number of young people saying the Rosary, not just in formal groups at these official hours but also along the wayside sitting in the sun or wherever they happened to be.

We even got into the habit of saying the Rosary as we walked along the road from one place to another and people would come to join us on the way. Tony always went everywhere with his pink Rosary in his hands. He could recite the Rosary and knew all the mysteries, although he was like a child. He could also recognise Jesus on the Cross. Every time he passed a crucifix he would say, 'That is Jesus.' How many of us can say that we recognise Jesus every time we see Him? As in Matthew 25:31–46, Jesus says, 'For I was hungry and you gave me food; I was thirsty and you gave me drink; I was a stranger and you made me welcome; naked and you clothed me, sick and you visited me; in prison and you came to see me.'

And they asked, 'When did we see you hungry, thirsty, naked, a stranger, sick and in prison and go to see you?'

Jesus said, 'In so far as you did this to one of the least of my brothers or sisters, you did it to me.'

Tony certainly made us feel humble; he always recognised Jesus.

Love and Peace

(MIR)

Chapter Two

MEDJUGORJE CONTINUED

On Sunday, 26 May 1991 we left Heathrow for Medjugorje. We were originally booked on a chartered flight from Stansted airport to Split in what was then Yugoslavia, but because of the civil war there, we were not allowed to go to Split.

Instead we went by Yugoslav Airways to Belgrade and from there flew to Mostar Airport. We were supposed to leave Heathrow at 12.30 a.m. but were delayed one hour because a coach carrying fifty male voice singers from Wales who were supposed to be on our flight had broken down on the motorway. When they eventually arrived, however, we took off.

At this point in our journey we were each given a small wooden cross with someone's name on it, and we were to carry their cross and pray for them on the pilgrimage. We each knew whose cross we were carrying, but did not know who was carrying our own. I will tell you more about these crosses later.

Before we reached Belgrade the pilot said we would be landing at Zagreb first. We duly arrived at Zagreb and had to disembark. After our luggage was taken off the plane and checked once again, we were allowed to re-board, but the singers did not return, so that must have been their destination. From Zagreb we flew to Belgrade where we changed planes for Mostar. At Mostar Airport we were met by our courier, Bernard, a young Yugoslav boy from Medjugorje. It was about 11.30 p.m. when we arrived at the house we were to stay in, where a lovely meal had been prepared for us, and our hosts made us most welcome. We were all glad to get to bed.

We awoke the next morning to pouring rain. Our first engagement of the day was to meet Vicka outside her house about a mile away. We walked though the rain and joined the crowd which had gathered there. We said five decades of the Rosary with Vicka and then she spoke to us through an interpreter. She answered our questions and was smiling all the time. We did not know then, but were later told, that she had a brain tumour. When a priest asked her if Our Lady would cure her, Vicka replied, 'She did not say and I wouldn't ask her because I'm offering my pain for sinners.' Our Lady, however, promised her, 'Because of your patient suffering I am going to bring about a great good.'

By the time we got back to the house we were saturated. After changing, we were off to the 10 a.m. Mass at the parish church of Medjugorje, which is Saint James' (Saint James was the first Bishop of Jerusalem). This was the Mass for the English-speaking people, and the church was packed with English, Americans, Australians, Irish and people from all English-speaking countries. Over thirty priests concelebrated the Mass. There was a tremendous feeling of unity and belonging. The Mass was said by an American priest, a big man over six feet tall and in his sixties. He started his homily by telling us about a man called Fred. Fred was the youngest son of a family of seven children. He was an alcoholic and a drug user, and the despair of his parents. Then he heard about Medjugorje, visited it and returned home a changed man. He was in his late fifties then, and went into training and a few years later became a priest. He finished by saying simply, 'I am Fred.' The clapping that followed was deafening. At the 'Our Father', everyone in the church held hands with their neighbour on either side, and at 'Give us this day our daily bread,' we all raised our hands up. It made us feel that the church was truly universal when we held the hand of someone from the other side of the world.

After the Mass we were to meet another of the visionaries, Ivan, in the marquee not far from the church. When we arrived there, a healing service was in progress, given by an Irish priest. I decided to take my mother up to him, so joined the queue of people waiting for him to lay his hands on them. After he had blessed her and spoken to her for a short time, he asked me to sit on a bench next to him. He laid his hands on my head and said, 'I am getting a message for you. You are to read Revelations 21.' I read it when I got back and it was about the Jerusalem of the future – 'then I saw a new Heaven and a new Earth.' You must read this yourself.

After the healing service Ivan arrived. He spoke to us for about an hour through an interpreter, and told us about Our Lady's messages. He told us again what Our Lady wants of us: prayer of the Rosary and prayer of the heart, the Eucharist, the Bible, fasting and monthly confession. Our Lady still appears to the visionaries: to four of them every day, to one of them once a year on her birthday, and to Marija on every 25th of the month to give her the messages for the world. After Ivan had spoken, we had a question and answer session, and one of the questions that everyone wanted answered was, 'What did Our Lady look like when she appeared?'

Ivan said, 'She was dressed in a grey robe with a white veil. She has dark hair, blue eyes and rosy cheeks, and has a crown of twelve stars around her head. But on special days like the Assumption she appears dressed in gold.' The first time Our Lady appeared to the visionaries she was also carrying the baby Jesus. The visionaries, as she would later remind them, ran away. How frequently we run from the one we need the most – Mary's Son.

Once, two years previously on Good Friday, she appeared with Jesus crowned with thorns and said, 'Look at my Beloved Son still martyred in the world.' When Ivan was relating the experience to an interviewer from the Sunday Times, so revolting was the memory that he had to turn away. Ivan had described the horror of the scene: the face of Christ was running with blood. 'We could see the thorns being pushed through the skin on his forehead.' Ivan also told us that Our Lady would appear to him on Apparition Hill at 10 a.m. that night and that everyone was invited to come.

After meeting Ivan we were free to look around, have lunch, and do any shopping we might wish. We were advised to buy our religious objects from the Franciscan repository (all the priests in Yugoslavia are Franciscans). We were free until 3 p.m. when Father Jozo was going to talk to us in the church. When the apparitions first started, Father Jozo was the parish priest of Saint James'. He was later sent to prison for supporting the apparitions and subsequently removed from any future position at Saint James' as a condition of his release. We were all really looking forward to meeting him, as we had already heard and read so much about him. Our Lady says of him, 'Father Jozo is already a saint.' We were not disappointed. Father Jozo Dovico is a handsome and idealistic Franciscan in his early forties, and although he speaks no English, and only spoke through an interpreter, we were spellbound. He was supposed to have spoken to us for one hour, but talked for two and a half. Nobody noticed the time. He never uses notes but speaks straight from the heart.

Father Jozo said, 'Only a few priests in this area speak English. I am sad that I don't speak English. When we went to school, we thought that the United States was so far from our country that we would never see an American in our lives. We learned German, French, Italian and Russian, and now we are sad that we don't speak English. I can't hear your confession, but I can celebrate Mass for you.'

On the subject of Americans, people say that they have the biggest bank balances, the biggest cars and unkindly the biggest mouths, but at Medjugorje the Americans, both priests and pilgrims, shone out as the people with the biggest hearts.

Love and Peace

(MIR)

Chapter Three

FATHER JOZO

Continuing the talk given to us in the Church of Saint James in Medjugorje by Father Jozo on Monday, 27 May 1991, he said: 'It is an interesting experience for us all here in Medjugorje that languages are not separating us. There is another language, a language that is uniting us all and that we all understand well. It is the language of prayer.'

He went on to tell us that when the apparitions started on 24 June 1981 he did not believe the visionaries: 'I remember how determined and inflexible they were in the first days. I remember how they made me lose sleep at night and I had no peace. They even made me feel inadequate. I found it difficult to believe the children. I was afraid that people might ridicule the Church. I couldn't believe that the children could have a conversation with Our Lady. Their parents did not believe them and I didn't believe them. But they believed within themselves and they kept repeating the same things every day.

'Then the persecution began, but the children endured. I remember they came running from the police. I was in the church by myself praying. I was saddened by the behaviour of the parishioners, who left the church to go to Apparition Mountain. I began to pray very sincerely for I was troubled: "Lord, what if the people going to the Mountain are really offending you? You gave signs to Moses on how to lead his people. I want to be on your side. I don't want these people to be deceived here."

'Then I heard a voice while I was praying. It said to me, "Go out and protect the children." I was sitting in the third pew on the right and Our Lady's statue stood before me. Without a second thought I got up and walked out. The children came running from the left side, out of breath, frightened, and swarmed around me like bees saying, "Protect us. The police are after us." I took them into a room in the rectory and locked the door. I went outside and sat under a tree and the police came running up to me asking, "Did you see the children?" I said yes, and they kept running in the direction of Bijakovici, the village where the children are from. That day was the first time the children had the apparition in the rectory.

'It was the next day after Mass that Our Lady came to the church. Until that day I did not believe. Our Lady came and made herself known to us, so when I actually received the Grace, thanks to God and Our Lady, I started to listen over and over again to the tapes on which everything was recorded from the first day. I listened to the words of the children but with much hope, certainty and beauty. The children were not extensively educated in faith but were just like anyone else in the village; they were not outstanding in any way. But now they live the kind of life that even some of the clergy would find difficult.'

Father Jozo went on to say: 'It is the fruits of many conversions that we recognise here in Medjugorje, the conversion of our human hearts, the grace of conversion and changes in us who were full of selfishness, and the readiness of the people to live the message of peace. I remember when we saw the word MIR (Peace) written in big, burning letters in the sky over Mount Križevac (Cross Mountain). We were shocked! The moment passed but we were unable to speak. No one dared say a word. Slowly, we came to our senses. We realised that we were still alive. The word MIR was blazing in our hearts. I felt that there was not a person present who didn't want to live that peace.

'After that, there wasn't a person who was not peaceful. There wasn't a family that lived in unrest. You see, that is very important; people began to want peace, to make peace and live peace. This is a fruit which cannot be produced by men of politics, by men of arms or by means of force. Only the Son of God can give peace and with it nourish the Church and the entire world.

'Our Lady would not have been able to express herself fully if she had only left the word MIR in the sky along with other visible signs. There would be something left out and everyone would imagine different things. She reached out for something concrete. She found for herself those of the village who were most simple, those whom other people would probably never choose. But she, as a mother, chose just those – the little ones, the seers (visionaries). The children were stubborn and knew how to suffer for the truth, and later became great apostles, apostles whom Our Lady used, through their meekness and weakness, to proclaim the great name of Jesus and to distribute their gifts.'

Father Jozo went on to tell us about his arrest: 'On 17 August 1981 the expected visit came and I was arrested. My going to prison was no accident but it had nothing to do with being stubborn or provoking the authorities. It was the logical result of the choices we all make at some stage in our lives. Every good priest should see the inside of a jail and suffer for the faith. I discovered in prison what the Catholic Faith is, and the strength and dignity of a life being offered.

'During the first weeks of the apparitions, Ivan had said to me, "The only ones who do not believe us are the priests and the police." The events had come full circle. On 22 October 1981 I was sentenced to three years in prison. At the same time, two other Franciscans, Father Ferdo Viasic and Jozo Krizic, were also given multiple-year sentences for contributing to the alleged uprising.

'It was not only me who went to prison; people were going before and after me. It didn't bother us at all! We were joyful – we felt that it should be that way.'

Father Jozo continued: 'Prison locks are as nothing against God's power. No one can take faith away, nor deny the action of grace. You cannot truly imprison anyone who believes. At the very moment when he has lost everything, he finds greatest strength.'

Strong pressure was brought to bear on the government and hundreds of letters, many of them from outside Yugoslavia, obtained a reduction of Father Jozo's sentence. He was released from prison in the spring of 1983, after eighteen months' imprisonment.

Father Jozo said, 'I did not remain long at Saint James' parish in Medjugorje after my return. It was one of the conditions of my release. The apparitions, by this time, had attracted worldwide attention. Millions were making their way to the remote village. Moreover, Bishop Zanic changed his original favourable opinion of the events and had emerged as the prime adversary and antagonist.

'I was transferred and became Pastor of Saint Elijah's Church in Tihaljina, some fifteen to twenty miles from Medjugorje.' (This church is now called the Church of the Immaculate Conception.)

Before Father Jozo left he told us again of the five things that Our Lady is asking of us at Medjugorje. 'I give you the weapon,' he said. 'Here are your five stones: prayer of the Rosary, prayer of the heart; Eucharist; Bible; fasting; and finally, monthly confession.'

He likened the stones to the five stones that David the shepherd carried in his pouch when he confronted Goliath. And by the stones he won the victory. We all know what happened to David! Father Jozo then asked us to pray for his country. He said there was great trouble there, although you would never know from the peace in Medjugorje. In fact, the whole nine days we were there, we only saw one police car pass through the village. We were quite surprised because there were four thousand pilgrims there at that time. Father Jozo also invited us to his church in Tihaljina on Thursday which was the feast of Corpus Christi, and he would say Mass for all the English-speaking people.

Of course we were all late back for our evening meal, which we ate very quickly because we wanted to be back in time to say the Rosary at 6 p.m. in the church.

Love and Peace
(MIR)

P.S. Not long after writing this chapter, the troubles in Yugoslavia have come to a head. But as Father Slavko Barbavic OFM, a leading Franciscan in Medjugorje, said to us at Aylesford at the end of August, 'This is not an ethnic issue – it is much deeper than that. It is about *freedom.*'

Chapter Four

OUR LADY

The Rosary had started when we arrived at Saint James' Church just after 6 p.m. We were all in an expectant mood, because we had been told when the Rosary is said in the church in the evening, and the visionaries are there, Our Lady is in the church with us.

Father Slavko was leading the Rosary and the responses were being said in eighteen different languages. We did not know the words the other people were using but we all knew what they were saying. As the time approached for Our Lady to appear, a certain hush came over the whole church although we were still saying the responses. Suddenly a teenager who was paralysed and in a wheelchair and could not speak, started screaming. She had been quiet all day at other services, but now she was in a very agitated state. This went on for some time. Father Slavko stopped leading the Rosary and all the church was quiet, as her mother took her outside. We never knew if she had seen Our Lady because she could not tell anyone, but we know Our Lady was in the church; the time seemed to stand still. Later – it seemed much later – Father Slavko resumed the Rosary. This was followed by celebration of the Holy Mass in Croatian (which happens every evening) and is an experience that will never be forgotten. Our Lady has said, 'Make heaven your goal,' and in Medjugorje she truly shows us how.

Many people go to Medjugorje looking for signs and wonders; such phenomena are to be found there, but one should not go seeking things of this nature. These are special little gifts from God to His children to help them on their journey of faith. He is Our Father and knows our needs. If we go to Him with an open heart, He can work wonders within us, and it is in these greater miracles within the hearts of his people that He will change the world, and bring about His Kingdom.

We walked home in darkness after Mass, no one wanting to speak, not wanting to spoil the experience of the evening. It is in the quiet that we really hear the voice of God: 'Be still and know that I am God.'

When we got back to our guest house David (pronounced *Dar-vid*) and his wife made us tea, and we sat talking about the day as we waited for it to be time to go to Apparition Hill (in Podbrdo). Ivan had said that Our Lady would appear at 12 a.m. and everyone who was going wanted to be there in good time. Bernard, our courier, was coming to lead us up the mountain. We all took torches as it was already dark. As we walked the mile to the foot of the mountain, crowds were joining us on the way. As everyone was walking at a different pace our group was soon split up, but we just followed the person in front of us. The climb was rocky and quite difficult but I eventually got to the top. It is here that Our Lady, or the

'Gospa' as she is known here, first appeared. There is a cross to mark the spot. On the way up the mountain the route was indicated by five plaques representing the five joyful mysteries of the Rosary.

While we waited for 12 a.m. to come, we prayed the Rosary and sang hymns. There was a group of young people with guitars leading the singing. We all managed to find a rock to sit on, or a place to kneel. My companions that night were a lady from Birmingham and two boys from Detroit. It was pitch dark apart from out torches and the light from candles around the cross. As it neared 12 a.m. the clouds parted and an enormous full moon appeared almost above the cross. We were told to look at the cross and nobody was to take photographs.

We knew Our Lady was talking to Ivan. There was complete silence. As we watched, the cross was hit by shafts of light. This went on for about half an hour. Many of us had different experiences at that time; mine was an overpowering smell of roses while sitting on that barren hillside.

After Our Lady had left us, Ivan's interpreter told us what Our Lady had said, and finished by saying that she sent a special blessing for everyone who was on the mountain that night. We stayed a little while longer and prayed in silence. Then it was time to make our descent. It was much harder going down than going up; as people lost their footing on the slippery rocks in the darkness they were grabbing their neighbours, who were in fact complete strangers. As I said before, our group had been split up and so had many others.

It was dark again as the moon had gone behind the

clouds, and we had left the village behind. There were no lights on the country roads. At every corner I turned, I wondered if I was going in the right direction. At last I saw a building which I recognised as being the corner of the turning to our house – home at last. I went into our kitchen/dining room where the other members of our group who had not gone to Apparition Hill were gathered. Monica (who had a bad back) had to turn back before we got to the hill, but that morning she had telephoned London and learned that she had a new grandson. On the kitchen table were six bottles of champagne that Clive, the pilgrimage organiser from the Centre for Peace, had brought. He happened to be in Medjugorje on business for a few days, and received a fax giving him the news. What a fantastic first day in Medjugorje: we had been in Our Lady's presence twice; we had met Vicka, Ivan, Marija and Father Jozo; we had been to Holy Mass twice, and prayed the Rosary many times. And then we drank six bottles of champagne.

Love and Peace

(MIR)

P.S. At Medjugorje Our Lady has asked us to keep 25 June, the day following the Feast of Saint John the Baptist, and the date of the first apparition, as a feast of Our Lady Queen of Peace. The 25th of each month is also the day Our Lady gives Marija the message for the world. Here is the message Our Lady gave on 25 June 1991 to the visionary Marija Pavlovic for the village of Medjugorje and the world:

> 'Dear children! Today on the great day which you have given to me, I desire to bless all of you and say, these days while I am with you are days of grace. I desire to teach you and to help you on the path to holiness. There are many people who don't desire to understand my messages and to accept with seriousness what I am saying, but you I therefore call, and ask that by your lives and your daily living you witness my presence.
>
> 'If you pray, God will help you to discover the true reason for my coming. Therefore, little children, pray and read the sacred scriptures so that through my coming you discover the message in sacred scripture for you.
>
> 'Thank you for having responded to my call.'

Chapter Five

MOUNT KRIŽEVAC – CROSS MOUNTAIN

I have not skipped Tuesday because nothing special happened – it was just as eventful as Monday – but I want to tell you a couple more things before I wind up. If you go to Medjugorje you are asked to go back home and tell as many people as you can about the village and Our Lady's messages. It is not to remain a one-to-one encounter. Like the parable of the 'talents' (Matthew 25:14–30), we are not to be like the man who was given one talent, and hid it in the ground, and there it remained as one talent, but we must be like the man who was given five talents. He went and traded them and made five more. What do we do with the talents we are given? Do we share them with other people? Everyone has been given a gift which is unique to his or her self. As a meditation by Venerable Cardinal John Henry Newman says, 'God has created me to do Him some definite service. He has committed some work to me which He has not committed to another. I have my mission – I am a link in a chain, a bond of connection between persons…'

And when the Master returned, what did he say to the servant who had hidden the 'talent' in the ground? In Medjugorje, Mary our Mother is alerting us to our own annunciations – all the messages she is giving us there and all the calls we receive from God through our consciences – she wishes us to answer, as she did, with generous surrender to God's Holy Spirit.

The hymn we had chosen as our own personal pilgrimage hymn was 'Walk with Me O my Lord'. We sang this every morning after the 'Morning Offering' in the dining room, before breakfast. Those of you who attended the Women's World Day of Prayer service in 1991 may remember that this was also one of the hymns the Women of Kenya chose to accompany the theme 'On Our Journey Together'. Once we had sung this hymn we felt set up for the day, knowing that Jesus would walk with us in whatever came our way. It certainly came into its own on the day in question (especially the words 'stones often bar my path and there are times we fall'), for this was the day we were to climb Cross Mountain – Mount Križevac.

About one kilometre as the crow flies from the church of Medjugorje rises the hill of Crnica, a continuation of Mount Križevac, and where they meet they make an angle. Mount Križevac is 520 metres (1716 feet) above sea level and commands a breathtaking view of the whole of Brotnjo, Namija and part of Bekija. The hill was called Sipovac until 1933, when it was named Križevac (*kriz* means cross) at the proposal of the parish priest of Medjugorje, Father Bernardin Smoljan. In that year the priest and inhabitants of Medjugorje erected on its top an 8.56 metre (28 feet) high, reinforced concrete cross dedicated to 'Jesus Christ, the Redeemer of Mankind, as a mark of their faith, love and hope'. Carved on the cross itself is,

'To mark the 1,900th anniversary of the Passion of Jesus', as is noted in the parish chronicle.

It took only a month and a half to erect the cross. It was very difficult and demanded a lot of effort to take the building materials there. All this was overcome by the mutual love and concord between the inhabitants of Medjugorje. During the construction of the cross, the menfolk of the parish carried up all the materials – cement, sand, water, etc. – on their shoulders in memory of Christ's Way of the Cross (we could barely carry ourselves up the mountain). A relic of the True Cross is buried inside the cross on the mountain.

The message given by Our Lady on 30 August 1984 was, 'Dear children! The cross was also in God's plan when you built it. These days, especially, go on the mountain and pray before the cross. I need your prayers. Thank you for having responded to my call.'

The message on 6 September the same year ran: 'Dear children! Without prayer there is no peace. Therefore I say to you, dear children, pray at the foot of the cross for peace. Thank you for having responded to my call.'

When I first saw Mount Križevac and the Cross reaching the sky on top, I said I was not going to attempt to climb it (I have had enough trouble climbing the hills of Woodingdean for well over twenty years), but gradually one persuaded another until twelve out of sixteen had decided to go, saying if we couldn't make it to the top we would wait for the others to come back down. The temperature was now up in the nineties (Fahrenheit) after the rain of the first day, and that heat remained for the whole time we were there.

We almost had to tie Judi down to stop her going (she had her eighth child, a little boy, on 14 September). Sister Martine was going. She was in her sixties and had been in hospital following a heart attack from overwork two months before. Sister Eileen was also going; she was in her seventies and had been ill in bed two weeks before we set out on our pilgrimage. Frank, Anne and their mentally handicapped son Tony were going. Tony said he would walk for those who couldn't go: my mother, Alice who was in her seventies, Monica because of her bad back, and Judi. Monica and Judi would look after the two ladies who were in wheelchairs. Eric, also in his seventies, was going. Alice was not very happy about this, but we reassured her that Monica and Judi would look after her (and my mother), and we felt that Eric needed some space for himself, away from his constant but devoted vigil with Alice. He wasn't expecting to do this when he came and had not brought any suitable shoes, so he climbed Cross Mountain in his shiny black shoes – and he got to the top! Sarah was also going (a lovely Irish girl in her early twenties) with her baby daughter of fifteen months on her back. Then there was Margaret, our friend who was in her fifties, Anna our Italian lady, and Kitty who was Irish and a widow, both in their sixties, along with myself.

We were to start our climb at 10 a.m., and Bernard was going to lead us. We were going up the mountain with another group from Manchester. They had brought their own priest with them and he said Mass for us in the Adoration Chapel, not far from the Church of Saint James, at 9 a.m. After Mass we all gathered together and Bernard led us towards Cross Mountain.

Love and Peace
(MIR)

The Hill of the Cross, Križevac – the Cross of our Love

Chapter Six

CROSS MOUNTAIN CONTINUED

The immediate area around the church and in the village is flat. The soil is poor, but thanks to a hot summer and adequate rainfall, tobacco and vines are cultivated. The population of Medjugorje is between 2,500 and 3,000 people – about 450 families. They are Croat and Catholics, and this is their livelihood. The foot of Mount Križevac is about 1.5 miles from the Church of Saint James, so to reach it we walked beside fields of vines.

It is easy to see why Jesus spoke in parables to his people. He spoke to them about things that were part of their everyday lives. As in the parable of the vine: 'I am the true vine, and my Father is the vinedresser. Every branch of mine that bears no fruit, he takes away, and every vine that does bear fruit, he prunes, that it may bear more fruit – abide in me and I in you' (John 15:1–11). The gnarled roots of the vines producing young branches of green leaves, and later grapes, brings this parable home to you and the vital union which must exist between Christ and his followers. As each Christian is united with the same Christ as the source of his religious fruitfulness, all Christians are united with each other in the living communion of the assembly of Christ's followers. We all belong to one family, the family of God.

We were told about four hours should be allowed for the ascent of Cross Mountain and return to base. It took us five and a half hours. The path that leads up the mountain is steeper, more difficult and longer that the one leading to the Hill of the Apparitions. Križevac does not attract so many pilgrims because of its natural beauty, or because of the cross standing upon it, but because many people have seen various lights and other 'signs' on the cross connected with the apparitions of the Virgin (where Mary is, Jesus is found) and with the essential message of Medjugorje – peace between God and man and among men. They realised that the path to that peace had to lead through the cross. And so part of their pilgrimage became honouring the cross, especially the cross on Križevac. Climbing along the almost impossible path to the cross, they began to perform rites of the Way of the Cross. That is why fourteen simple crosses were placed beside the path leading up the hill of Križevac. The route is marked by fifteen beautiful Stations of the Cross – sculptured bronze plaques made in Italy. In the spring of 1988 these bronze reliefs were placed in the rocks beside those wooden crosses – fourteen stations of the Passion of Jesus and the Way of the Cross, and a fifteenth place under the cross itself showing the Resurrection. The reliefs were made by the Italian sculptor Carmelo Puzzolo, and financed by the Italian industrialists Brazzle and Dalle Carbondi. A special feature of these stations is that they all show the figure of the Virgin. Each relief weighs at least 150 kg, and they were carried and placed in position by young people of Medjugorje.

We had now reached the foot of Križevac and our pilgrimage began in earnest as we started to climb the path. We paired off to help each other. Sister Martina was helping Sister Eileen. Sister Eileen was seventy-six years old and at the end of November was given only a few days to live. We prayed for her in our Rosary groups. (When I was in London for my nephew's wedding a good deal later, on 14 December 1991, we saw Sister Eileen walk in to Sunday Mass unaccompanied.) Margaret and I paired off as a back-up team to anyone in real difficulties. Margaret was from the local Anglican Church in London.

We reached the first station and, while waiting for all our group to gather, a lady from Manchester led us in a Taizé until all had arrived, the words being 'All who pass this way, look and see.' We said the appropriate prayers and sung a hymn, and then moved on to the second station. Incidentally, I met the lady again at Aylesford last year.

As we ascended it seemed to be getting hotter and those women who were wearing sleeveless dresses against the heat began to look as red as lobsters. Kitty was having real difficulties with her breathing and we thought she was going to collapse. We helped her as best we could. She threw her bag she was carrying aside and said she would find it on the way down. Bernard went back and retrieved it when he heard, and he carried it for her. Sister Martina was having difficulty with Sister Eileen; she was literally carrying her over the rocks. A young American man coming up behind us and said he would help Sister Eileen and if we let him know when we were going back, he would help her down. Sarah was also getting some help in carrying her young daughter, who she had in a harness on her back. Two priests were taking it in turns to carry her. Margaret and I were going from one to another who needed a helping hand. Eric, in his seventies, was doing remarkably well in spite of his shiny black shoes. He suddenly seemed to have a new lease of life. Frank was helping his son Tony, and so on.

The view got more beautiful the higher we went, but there was no shade from the sun. We were beginning to feel something of Jesus' journey to Calvary: 'They tried to hasten his steps when he could scarcely move.' But of course we were not carrying a heavy wooden cross. Some members of our group were carrying crosses of a different kind though. Once we got past the pain barrier we were able to go a bit faster. At one of the stations a Bassett Hound was lying asleep; he usually lay at the feet of the statue of the Virgin not far from the church. Bernard said that one winter night when a mist suddenly came down and he was lost on the mountain, the dog had come and led him to safety.

At last we had reached the top of Cross Mountain and we made our way to the foot of the cross, where Mary had stood. We joined in with prayers and hymns that were being led by a group of Americans who were already there. The cross bore the inscription, in Croat: 'IHS (Jesus in Greek letters) 33–1933, to Jesus Christ the Redeemer of the human race. As a sign of their faith, hope and love, Pastor Bernardin Smoljan and the Parish of Medjugorje erected this Cross.' The triangle at the foot of the Cross reads: 'From every evil deliver us, O Jesus.'

You get a very strange feeling standing on top of the mountain as if you were standing on top of the world, and looking down on everything that was happening below. Although the temperature was still in the upper nineties, a cool breeze was blowing. We wondered what we were to take back down the mountain, and if Moses had felt like that when he came down Mount Sinai after receiving the Commandments, or Peter, James and John when they returned from the high mountain (Matthew 17:1–8). We had a good discussion about it that evening. Križevac is also known as 'the Cross of Our Love'.

Before returning down the mountain, we sat down for a rest and shared out our bottles of water and bread, as it was Wednesday, our fast day. The return journey was more difficult than coming up and there were a few nasty falls. The rocks were like polished marble from years of pilgrims' feet.

We arrived back at the Church of Saint James at exactly 3.30 p.m. But our pilgrimage was not yet over as we are a pilgrim people and a pilgrim church and our pilgrimage goes on until we see Him face to face.

Love and Peace

(MIR)

Chapter Seven

OBRACENJE (CONVERSION)

After climbing Mount Križevac, we arrived back at the Church of Saint James and were told that Marija was receiving pilgrims outside her house in the village from 3 p.m., which was some distance away. Sister Martina said we must go, as it might be the only opportunity we would get to see her. I could hardly put one foot in front of the other, so Sister Martina said she would push my mother's wheelchair. She took off her shoes and ran into the distance, pushing my mother's wheelchair. I said I would catch them up, but if I was never to see Marija I could not go any faster. I did eventually catch them up outside Marija's house, but on the way, every corner I turned, there was no one to be seen. My mother and Sister Martina had been to Medjugorje before so they knew the way to Marija's house. I just got there in time and was able to see her for a short while.

On Monday, 26 May 1991, Father Jozo had invited us to his Church of Saint Elijah in Tihaljina (now called the Church of the Immaculate Conception) for Thursday, 30 May, which was the Feast of Corpus Christi. This was also a great day for me as it was the Golden Jubilee of my Confirmation and first Holy

Communion (Corpus Christ, but not quite the same date, which was 15 June 1941). I was confirmed when I was six years old in the Church of the Holy Trinity in a little village called Hethe, near Bicester in Oxfordshire, where I had been evacuated after being bombed out in the Blitz in London in 1940. We were to be picked up by coach at 6.20 a.m. We had an early breakfast and Bernard arrived to accompany us. We were going with a couple of other groups and were the first to be picked up. We stopped at several different places to collect other pilgrims, some of them children.

The journey to Tihaljina passed quickly, through the little villages and over the mountains. In the villages there were blazes of colour. It was roses, especially red roses. In fact you thought you were in England, the roses grew so well there. We arrived at Father Jozo's church. We were one of the first groups to arrive, so we made our way up to the top of the church and took our seats on the left-hand side. We were seated in front of the beautiful statue of Our Lady in Saint Elijah's. The present church at Tihaljina was constructed in the 1960s. At the time the parish priest had visited Rome where he discovered and fell in love with this remarkable image of Our Lady. Since his new church was under construction he felt this newfound replica of Our Lady must become part of his parish. He ordered one, shipped from Rome. Something happened to delay the arrival of the statue (perhaps I will tell you something about that another time). But, now, over twenty years later, people from all over the world are enriched by its presence.

The Mass was beautiful, concelebrated by thirty or

more English-speaking priests. The Gospel began with the words, 'And Jesus called Matthew.' Then came Father Jozo's homily. As he spoke it was taken down by a young, beautiful Yugoslav girl. When he had finished she read this to us in English.

Although we did not understand the language, when Father Jozo spoke we seemed to understand what he meant. Obracenje (conversion) was his main theme, and the insight which Father Jozo presents is perhaps one of the most extraordinary. He seems to be able to express it in the simplest, yet most compelling ways. It is a difficult and often misunderstood word in our times.

Every time the seers are asked about the 'main message' of Our Lady. Their answers may vary in wording, but their meaning is always the same. In the words of Marija, 'All the messages concern the world, such as conversion, faith, peace, prayer, fasting and penance.'

Conversion, then, is a basic message from Medjugorje, and conversion is a basic message in all prophecy. Mary, as a special prophet of our times, calls and encourages all people to conversion. Earlier, Jeremiah also called his people to conversion, telling them, 'Cleanse your heart of evil' (Jer 4:14). Cleansing your heart from evil is conversion and Our Lady conveys that power of conversion from God to all peoples, to every person. It is not a message of fear or doom, but God's loving plan and desire to bring each person into His Kingdom. Thus Our Lady has become a prophetess for our time, a time which has lost touch with itself and with God. She wants to put us in touch again; therefore she has come to Medjugorje and to the world. That word, 'conversion' is the process she requests.

The unclean heart is the source of all our evil. Even in Ezekiel's time this judgement was rendered, for he told his people, 'As I live, says the Lord God, I swear I take no pleasure in the death of a wicked man, but in the wicked man's conversion, that he may live' (Ezekiel 33:10–11). How complicated we have made those words. Today, theologians provide endless volumes of material trying to unravel the mysteries of the Christ, His Church, His words, our salvation. In the process, we wind up trying to re-write the Gospels, modernise the Church and update the Commandments, all in an attempt to lay out the 'correct' means of salvation.

So it is with the word 'conversion'. Our self-appointed intellectualism of today tries to find new meaning, new processes, new ways of adaptation to incorporate conversion into our already complicated lives, and to our detriment. Father Jozo, on the other hand, reduces it to its simplest and purest terms in conveying the requests of Our Lady to her children. But as we drink in his thoughts, we suddenly became aware that is has all been said before. It has always been there. Father Jozo, as an instrument of Our Lord and Our Lady, simply brings out those basic truths, those same teachings which have somehow become clouded and obscured in a world too complicated for simple truths.

He points out the means of conversion are the Eucharist, prayer, penance, fasting and monthly confession. In response to Our Lady's call for conversion, many people have now resumed daily prayer, fasting and various forms of penance; long lines of penitent pilgrims have rediscovered the Sacrament of Reconciliation in Medjugorje.

Father Jozo states: 'It is prayer that Our Lady wants of us. The gift of prayer – for it is a special gift of God – is waiting to be born in you. Our Lady wants us to find salvation through Jesus. And we find Jesus through prayer, monthly confession, the Scriptures, Mass and fasting. All these things were already known to us, but we had stopped putting them into proper practice.

'Our Lady said, "I need your prayers. I need you. You are important – CONVERT!"

'I finally understood it all. She was talking to me. She is talking to you. She is telling me, "I want you to convert. Why are you trying to convert everyone else?" She does not say convert your family, your friends, your parishioners. Conversion is not adopting a certain religion. It is a process for each of us, individually. Peace begins within you. Love begins within you. Conversion begins within you and the world will never have these things until each of us individually finds this change of heart within ourselves; it is for each person, one at a time.

'This world doesn't need our selfishness, but our faith. This world doesn't need our pride, but our love. That is why the Church is a visible sign of the presence of God among people. Let us renew the Church! You are invited! Do not be afraid to answer the call. The one who invited you, walks with you; it is your God, who will not leave you; it is your

Mother who leads you and brings you along. Stay obedient.'

Father Jozo simply lives a definition of conversion in its purest form: make Jesus the most important part of your life – renew it every day. It originated from Our Lady, who always leads to Jesus. There are people who try to know Jesus by study. But to study theology, to study science, has only intellectual value. To love Jesus is another grace. It is a gift of love. One cannot love Jesus unless one prays. And he who doesn't pray, doesn't know Jesus.

I said previously that the Americans were the people with the biggest hearts at Medjugorje. Here is a little incident as evidence of what I mean. It was very difficult to get my mother on and off the coach that took us to Father Jozo's church in Tihaljina. When we arrived, there was an American couple who had come by taxi. They saw our difficulties and offered to return, after the service, to Medjugorje in our coach, so we could take their taxi. Because of their generosity we were able to see the Kravice Falls near Ljubuški – 'the eye wonders at splendour.' We were able to get quite close to the pool at the bottom of the waterfall, unlike the coach which was not able to come anywhere near the Falls because of the adverse terrain. Thanks to those two dear people, whose names we never knew, but met briefly, from the other side of the world. Truly Medjugorje is a meeting in love of the United Nations.

Love and Peace

(MIR)

Kravice Falls, near Ljubuški – 'the eye wonders at splendour'

Observations

―――◦○◦―――

*Observations on Medjugorje and the surrounding area.
From a book given out freely to those making the
pilgrimage to Medjugorje.*

MEDJUGORJE

'It is a call for the whole world
A call for people of good will
To find happiness and peace.
The day will come
When all of us will be as one
When you will be a true brother to me…
The day will come.'

Tomislav Ivčić

VILLAGE OF BIJAKOVICI

'It dreams that is has not
Tired of its old age
In my homeland stone
Blooms, too, and grapes
Ripe in autumn…'

Father Janico Bubato 'Antuila'

VILLAGE OF MILETINA

'…the colour of a
Pomegranate turned to
Stone, the memory of
Light at dawn…'

    Slavko Šantić, 'Dawn in Herzegovia'

ILLYRIAN HILL FORT OF ZUZELJ (ABOVE MEDJUGORJE)

'…that hill on which my eyes often rest
As I sit alone in my room!
Barren: it nurtures no life, only the bluish rocks.'

    A B Šimić, 'A Poem to a Hill'

'…the sun touched this sky long ago,
Now the gifts of the vine rustle in Herzegovina.'

    Slavko Šantić, 'Two Notes About Herzegovina'

'…the temple grows, the alter rises to the sky,
The priest elevates the sun to the blue heights.'

    Vladimir Nazor, 'Raising'

> 'And the circle of light should at last be entered…'
>
> Mark Dizdar, 'The Door'

> '…hands held in prayer.'

> '…let everything be one endless joy of stars and flowers.'
>
> A B Šimić, 'Prayer'

PRAYERS ON THE SITE OF THE VISION

'Joy in the heart, happiness in the soul'

> Podbrdo – the site of the vision

'Hands full of Sun'

> Pilgrims to Podbrdo

'The place where all nations meet, and here become one heart and one soul at the source of love and faith…'

> Pilgrims climbing Križevac

'And thus were the paths of those on earth made straight'

> (WISD 9–18)

'The way of the Cross – the first station
The Judgement of Jesus
The path to peace…'

'The red flowers of love burn in the night'
> A B Šimić 'The First Night of Solitude'

'A hand. This hand tells you to stop and think about your own hands.'
> Mark Dizdar, 'Radimja'

Love and Peace
(MIR)

Epilogue

We returned from Medjugorje on Monday, 3 June 1991. We were not to return home the same way as we came, but had to travel to Dubrovnik in the south to board an aeroplane. Leaving our house where we had stayed, we set out by mini-bus. It was still dark – about five o'clock in the morning. We travelled over the mountains and then witnessed the sunrise as we travelled down the coast of the Adriatic. It was so beautiful, the sea shinning a bright blue to the right of us. And of course we all sang the lovely hymn 'I Watch the Sunrise'.

When we got to the airport it was a bit stressful. We had to wait hours for a plane to take us back to Heathrow. We thought we would have to wait until the following day as the army had commandeered all the aeroplanes, and they said that they were only booked to take one lady in a wheelchair. We eventually persuaded them to take two – my mother and Alice.

We arrived back in England tired but exhilarated by our experience. I told you at the beginning of this account that we were each given a little wooden cross with someone's name on it before we set off, and we were to pray for that person throughout the pilgrimage. I had been given Sarah's cross and returned it to her, giving a little summary of what had struck me about her on the pilgrimage. Eric and Alice together had been carrying mine, and it was interesting to hear what they had to say about me. It is strange, sometimes, how other people see you, but helps you grow if they have seen something in you that you had never known in yourself. If you are going to Medjugorje, besides road, rail and air, Medjugorje can always be reached by the roads of the heart; 'You know those paths that start from the heart' (Mark Dizdar, 'Paths').

Love and Peace

(MIR)

With thanks to my dear mother,
Mrs Jennie Newley,
from your ever-loving daughter
Mrs Pamela Hill (née Pamela Jean Newley)